BIBLE JOURNAL FOR WOMEN

Bible Journal

FOR WOMEN

A Simple Study Companion
to Track Your Engagement
with Scripture

LaJena James

ROCKRIDGE
PRESS

First Rockridge Press trade paperback edition 2022

Rockridge Press and the Rockridge Press logo are trademarks or registered trademarks of Callisto Media Inc. and/or its affiliates in the United States and other countries and may not be used without written permission.

For general information on our other products and services, please contact our Customer Care Department within the United States at (866) 744-2665, or outside the United States at (510) 253-0500.

Paperback ISBN: 978-1-68539-283-3

Manufactured in the United States of America

Interior and Cover Designer: Scott Petrower
Art Producer: Megan Baggott
Editor: Kahlil Thomas
Production Editor: Emily Sheehan
Production Manager: Riley Hoffman

Photography © titoOnz/Shutterstock

Author photo courtesy of KLY Photography

10 9 8 7 6 5 4 3 2 1 0

This book belongs to

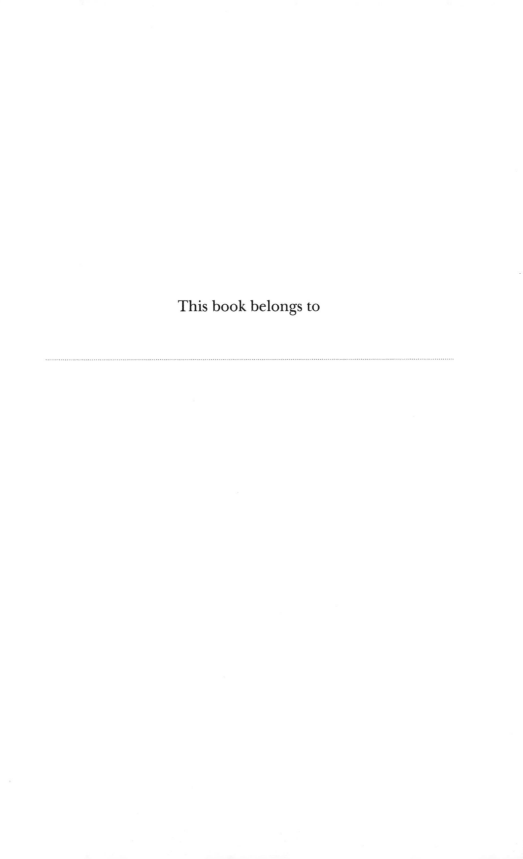

Introduction

One of my favorite things to do is journaling. I grew up writing all my thoughts in the pages of colorful *Lisa Frank* diaries. And when I became serious about studying God's Word during college, it was only in my true nature to pen my thoughts from each study on paper.

Over the last fifteen years, I've been mentoring women on how to study the Bible through journaling, which has helped them more deeply reflect during their study time and strengthen their connection to God. Journaling has also helped me as I serve as a pastor's wife, women's ministry leader, speaker, author, and coach for Christian women and girls.

My prayer is that by using this journal you will be challenged as a believer in your faith to understand God's Word for yourself and apply it to your life daily through your revelations.

This journal is divided into a 52-week format. Each week contains a verse citation to inspire reflection in case you're not sure where to begin. You have the option of referencing it or of visiting any other Bible readings you want—the choice is yours. Each week also contains templated prompts and questions to help you reflect on your reading for the week.

Use this Bible journal as a commitment to your relationship with God through His Word so that you can become a better you *and* a better believer.

-LaJena

For Inspiration: **Ephesians 2:8–9**

WEEK 1

Date ....

Cite the Scripture you read this week:

_____

_____

_____

_____

_____

_____

_____

How did your reading this week make you feel?

_____

_____

_____

_____

_____

_____

_____

_____

What lessons did you learn, and how can you apply them to your life?

....

....

....

....

....

....

What are some key takeaways from your reading this week?

....

....

....

....

....

....

....

Record your favorite verses from your reading this week:

_____

_____

_____

_____

_____

_____

_____

_____

Write a prayer inspired by what you read and learned this week:

_____

_____

_____

_____

_____

_____

_____

_____

_____

_____

WEEK 2

Date ....

Cite the Scripture you read this week:

....

....

....

....

....

....

....

....

How did your reading this week make you feel?

....

....

....

....

....

....

....

....

What lessons did you learn, and how can you apply them to your life?

_____

_____

_____

_____

_____

_____

_____

What are some key takeaways from your reading this week?

_____

_____

_____

_____

_____

_____

_____

_____

Record your favorite verses from your reading this week:

.

Write a prayer inspired by what you read and learned this week:

WEEK 3

Date ....

Cite the Scripture you read this week:

....

....

....

....

....

....

....

....

How did your reading this week make you feel?

....

....

....

....

....

....

....

....

What lessons did you learn, and how can you apply them to
your life?

....

....

....

....

....

....

....

What are some key takeaways from your reading this week?

....

....

....

....

....

....

....

....

Record your favorite verses from your reading this week:

....

....

....

....

....

....

....

....

Write a prayer inspired by what you read and learned this week:

....

....

....

....

....

....

....

....

WEEK 4

Date ....

Cite the Scripture you read this week:

....

....

....

....

....

....

....

....

How did your reading this week make you feel?

....

....

....

....

....

....

....

....

....

What lessons did you learn, and how can you apply them to your life?

_____

_____

_____

_____

_____

_____

_____

What are some key takeaways from your reading this week?

_____

_____

_____

_____

_____

_____

_____

_____

Record your favorite verses from your reading this week:

_____

_____

_____

_____

_____

_____

_____

_____

Write a prayer inspired by what you read and learned this week:

_____

_____

_____

_____

_____

_____

_____

_____

_____

WEEK 5

Date ....

Cite the Scripture you read this week:

....

....

....

....

....

....

....

....

How did your reading this week make you feel?

....

....

....

....

....

....

....

....

What lessons did you learn, and how can you apply them to your life?

....

....

....

....

....

....

....

What are some key takeaways from your reading this week?

....

....

....

....

....

....

....

....

Record your favorite verses from your reading this week:

....

....

....

....

....

....

....

....

Write a prayer inspired by what you read and learned this week:

....

....

....

....

....

....

....

....

....

WEEK 6

Date ....

Cite the Scripture you read this week:

....

....

....

....

....

....

....

....

How did your reading this week make you feel?

....

....

....

....

....

....

....

....

....

What lessons did you learn, and how can you apply them to your life?

....

....

....

....

....

....

....

What are some key takeaways from your reading this week?

....

....

....

....

....

....

....

....

Record your favorite verses from your reading this week:

....

....

....

....

....

....

....

Write a prayer inspired by what you read and learned this week:

....

....

....

....

....

....

....

....

For Inspiration: Genesis 1:26–27

WEEK 7

Date ....

Cite the Scripture you read this week:

....

....

....

....

....

....

....

....

How did your reading this week make you feel?

....

....

....

....

....

....

....

....

....

What lessons did you learn, and how can you apply them to your life?

....

....

....

....

....

....

....

What are some key takeaways from your reading this week?

....

....

....

....

....

....

....

Record your favorite verses from your reading this week:

....

....

....

....

....

....

....

....

Write a prayer inspired by what you read and learned this week:

....

....

....

....

....

....

....

....

....

WEEK 8

Date ....

Cite the Scripture you read this week:

....

....

....

....

....

....

....

How did your reading this week make you feel?

....

....

....

....

....

....

....

....

What lessons did you learn, and how can you apply them to your life?

_____

_____

_____

_____

_____

_____

_____

What are some key takeaways from your reading this week?

_____

_____

_____

_____

_____

_____

_____

_____

Record your favorite verses from your reading this week:

....

....

....

....

....

....

....

....

Write a prayer inspired by what you read and learned this week:

....

....

....

....

....

....

....

....

WEEK 9

Date ....

Cite the Scripture you read this week:

....

....

....

....

....

....

....

....

How did your reading this week make you feel?

....

....

....

....

....

....

....

....

....

What lessons did you learn, and how can you apply them to your life?

....

....

....

....

....

....

....

What are some key takeaways from your reading this week?

....

....

....

....

....

....

....

Record your favorite verses from your reading this week:

_____
_____
_____
_____
_____
_____
_____
_____

Write a prayer inspired by what you read and learned this week:

_____
_____
_____
_____
_____
_____
_____
_____
_____

WEEK 10

Date ....

Cite the Scripture you read this week:

_____

_____

_____

_____

_____

_____

_____

_____

How did your reading this week make you feel?

_____

_____

_____

_____

_____

_____

_____

_____

_____

What lessons did you learn, and how can you apply them to your life?

....

....

....

....

....

....

....

....

What are some key takeaways from your reading this week?

....

....

....

....

....

....

....

....

Record your favorite verses from your reading this week:

....

....

....

....

....

....

....

Write a prayer inspired by what you read and learned this week:

....

....

....

....

....

....

....

....

WEEK 11

Date ....

Cite the Scripture you read this week:

....

....

....

....

....

....

....

....

How did your reading this week make you feel?

....

....

....

....

....

....

....

....

....

What lessons did you learn, and how can you apply them to your life?

....

....

....

....

....

....

....

What are some key takeaways from your reading this week?

....

....

....

....

....

....

....

Record your favorite verses from your reading this week:

....

....

....

....

....

....

....

....

Write a prayer inspired by what you read and learned this week:

....

....

....

....

....

....

....

....

....

WEEK 12

Date ....

Cite the Scripture you read this week:

....

....

....

....

....

....

....

How did your reading this week make you feel?

....

....

....

....

....

....

....

....

What lessons did you learn, and how can you apply them to your life?

_____
_____
_____
_____
_____
_____
_____

What are some key takeaways from your reading this week?

_____
_____
_____
_____
_____
_____
_____
_____

Record your favorite verses from your reading this week:

....
....
....
....
....
....
....
....

Write a prayer inspired by what you read and learned this week:

....
....
....
....
....
....
....
....

WEEK 13

Date ....

Cite the Scripture you read this week:

How did your reading this week make you feel?

What lessons did you learn, and how can you apply them to your life?

....

....

....

....

....

....

....

....

What are some key takeaways from your reading this week?

....

....

....

....

....

....

....

....

Record your favorite verses from your reading this week:

_____

_____

_____

_____

_____

_____

_____

_____

Write a prayer inspired by what you read and learned this week:

_____

_____

_____

_____

_____

_____

_____

_____

WEEK 14

Date ....

Cite the Scripture you read this week:

....

....

....

....

....

....

....

How did your reading this week make you feel?

....

....

....

....

....

....

....

....

What lessons did you learn, and how can you apply them to
your life?

....

....

....

....

....

....

....

What are some key takeaways from your reading this week?

....

....

....

....

....

....

....

....

Record your favorite verses from your reading this week:

....

....

....

....

....

....

....

Write a prayer inspired by what you read and learned this week:

....

....

....

....

....

....

....

....

WEEK 15

Date ....

Cite the Scripture you read this week:

....

....

....

....

....

....

....

....

How did your reading this week make you feel?

....

....

....

....

....

....

....

....

....

What lessons did you learn, and how can you apply them to your life?

....

....

....

....

....

....

....

....

What are some key takeaways from your reading this week?

....

....

....

....

....

....

....

....

....

Record your favorite verses from your reading this week:

....
....
....
....
....
....
....
....

Write a prayer inspired by what you read and learned this week:

....
....
....
....
....
....
....
....
....

WEEK 16

Date ....

Cite the Scripture you read this week:

....

....

....

....

....

....

....

....

How did your reading this week make you feel?

....

....

....

....

....

....

....

....

....

What lessons did you learn, and how can you apply them to
your life?

....

....

....

....

....

....

....

What are some key takeaways from your reading this week?

....

....

....

....

....

....

....

Record your favorite verses from your reading this week:

....

....

....

....

....

....

....

....

Write a prayer inspired by what you read and learned this week:

....

....

....

....

....

....

....

....

WEEK 17

Date ....

Cite the Scripture you read this week:

....
....
....
....
....
....
....
....

How did your reading this week make you feel?

....
....
....
....
....
....
....
....
....

What lessons did you learn, and how can you apply them to your life?

....

....

....

....

....

....

....

What are some key takeaways from your reading this week?

....

....

....

....

....

....

....

....

Record your favorite verses from your reading this week:

....

....

....

....

....

....

....

....

Write a prayer inspired by what you read and learned this week:

....

....

....

....

....

....

....

....

....

WEEK 18

Date ....

Cite the Scripture you read this week:

....

....

....

....

....

....

....

....

How did your reading this week make you feel?

....

....

....

....

....

....

....

....

What lessons did you learn, and how can you apply them to your life?

....

....

....

....

....

....

....

....

What are some key takeaways from your reading this week?

....

....

....

....

....

....

....

....

Record your favorite verses from your reading this week:

....

....

....

....

....

....

....

Write a prayer inspired by what you read and learned this week:

....

....

....

....

....

....

....

....

WEEK 19

Date ....

Cite the Scripture you read this week:

....

....

....

....

....

....

....

....

How did your reading this week make you feel?

....

....

....

....

....

....

....

....

....

....

What lessons did you learn, and how can you apply them to your life?

....

....

....

....

....

....

....

What are some key takeaways from your reading this week?

....

....

....

....

....

....

....

....

Record your favorite verses from your reading this week:

....

....

....

....

....

....

....

....

Write a prayer inspired by what you read and learned this week:

....

....

....

....

....

....

....

....

....

WEEK 20

Date ....

Cite the Scripture you read this week:

....

....

....

....

....

....

....

How did your reading this week make you feel?

....

....

....

....

....

....

....

....

What lessons did you learn, and how can you apply them to your life?

....

....

....

....

....

....

....

What are some key takeaways from your reading this week?

....

....

....

....

....

....

....

....

Record your favorite verses from your reading this week:

....

....

....

....

....

....

....

Write a prayer inspired by what you read and learned this week:

....

....

....

....

....

....

....

....

WEEK 21

Date ....

Cite the Scripture you read this week:

....

....

....

....

....

....

....

....

How did your reading this week make you feel?

....

....

....

....

....

....

....

....

....

....

What lessons did you learn, and how can you apply them to your life?

_____

_____

_____

_____

_____

_____

_____

_____

What are some key takeaways from your reading this week?

_____

_____

_____

_____

_____

_____

_____

_____

Record your favorite verses from your reading this week:

....

....

....

....

....

....

....

....

Write a prayer inspired by what you read and learned this week:

....

....

....

....

....

....

....

....

....

....

WEEK 22

Date ....

Cite the Scripture you read this week:

....

....

....

....

....

....

....

....

How did your reading this week make you feel?

....

....

....

....

....

....

....

....

What lessons did you learn, and how can you apply them to your life?

....

....

....

....

....

....

....

What are some key takeaways from your reading this week?

....

....

....

....

....

....

....

....

Record your favorite verses from your reading this week:

_____

_____

_____

_____

_____

_____

_____

_____

Write a prayer inspired by what you read and learned this week:

_____

_____

_____

_____

_____

_____

_____

_____

WEEK 23

Date ....

Cite the Scripture you read this week:

....

....

....

....

....

....

....

....

How did your reading this week make you feel?

....

....

....

....

....

....

....

....

....

What lessons did you learn, and how can you apply them to your life?

....

....

....

....

....

....

....

What are some key takeaways from your reading this week?

....

....

....

....

....

....

....

....

Record your favorite verses from your reading this week:

....

....

....

....

....

....

....

....

Write a prayer inspired by what you read and learned this week:

....

....

....

....

....

....

....

....

....

WEEK 24

Date ....

Cite the Scripture you read this week:

....

....

....

....

....

....

....

....

How did your reading this week make you feel?

....

....

....

....

....

....

....

....

....

What lessons did you learn, and how can you apply them to your life?

....

....

....

....

....

....

....

What are some key takeaways from your reading this week?

....

....

....

....

....

....

....

....

Record your favorite verses from your reading this week:

....

....

....

....

....

....

....

Write a prayer inspired by what you read and learned this week:

....

....

....

....

....

....

....

WEEK 25

Date ....

Cite the Scripture you read this week:

....

....

....

....

....

....

....

How did your reading this week make you feel?

....

....

....

....

....

....

....

....

....

What lessons did you learn, and how can you apply them to your life?

....

....

....

....

....

....

....

What are some key takeaways from your reading this week?

....

....

....

....

....

....

....

....

Record your favorite verses from your reading this week:

....

....

....

....

....

....

....

....

Write a prayer inspired by what you read and learned this week:

....

....

....

....

....

....

....

....

....

WEEK 26

Date ....

Cite the Scripture you read this week:

....

....

....

....

....

....

....

....

How did your reading this week make you feel?

....

....

....

....

....

....

....

....

What lessons did you learn, and how can you apply them to your life?

....

....

....

....

....

....

....

What are some key takeaways from your reading this week?

....

....

....

....

....

....

....

....

Record your favorite verses from your reading this week:

....

....

....

....

....

....

....

Write a prayer inspired by what you read and learned this week:

....

....

....

....

....

....

....

WEEK 27

Date ....

Cite the Scripture you read this week:

....

....

....

....

....

....

....

How did your reading this week make you feel?

....

....

....

....

....

....

....

....

What lessons did you learn, and how can you apply them to your life?

_____

_____

_____

_____

_____

_____

_____

What are some key takeaways from your reading this week?

_____

_____

_____

_____

_____

_____

_____

_____

Record your favorite verses from your reading this week:

_____

_____

_____

_____

_____

_____

_____

Write a prayer inspired by what you read and learned this week:

_____

_____

_____

_____

_____

_____

_____

_____

WEEK 28

Date ....

Cite the Scripture you read this week:

....

....

....

....

....

....

....

....

How did your reading this week make you feel?

....

....

....

....

....

....

....

....

....

What lessons did you learn, and how can you apply them to your life?

_____

_____

_____

_____

_____

_____

_____

What are some key takeaways from your reading this week?

_____

_____

_____

_____

_____

_____

_____

_____

Record your favorite verses from your reading this week:

....

....

....

....

....

....

....

Write a prayer inspired by what you read and learned this week:

....

....

....

....

....

....

....

....

For Inspiration: Hosea 6:3

WEEK 29

Date ....

Cite the Scripture you read this week:

....

....

....

....

....

....

....

....

How did your reading this week make you feel?

....

....

....

....

....

....

....

....

What lessons did you learn, and how can you apply them to your life?

....

....

....

....

....

....

....

What are some key takeaways from your reading this week?

....

....

....

....

....

....

....

....

Record your favorite verses from your reading this week:

....

....

....

....

....

....

....

....

....

Write a prayer inspired by what you read and learned this week:

....

....

....

....

....

....

....

....

....

For Inspiration: Luke 6:38

WEEK 30

Date ....

Cite the Scripture you read this week:

....

....

....

....

....

....

....

....

How did your reading this week make you feel?

....

....

....

....

....

....

....

....

....

What lessons did you learn, and how can you apply them to your life?

....

....

....

....

....

....

....

What are some key takeaways from your reading this week?

....

....

....

....

....

....

....

....

Record your favorite verses from your reading this week:

_____

_____

_____

_____

_____

_____

_____

Write a prayer inspired by what you read and learned this week:

_____

_____

_____

_____

_____

_____

_____

_____

WEEK 31

Date ....

Cite the Scripture you read this week:

....

....

....

....

....

....

....

....

How did your reading this week make you feel?

....

....

....

....

....

....

....

....

....

What lessons did you learn, and how can you apply them to your life?

_____

_____

_____

_____

_____

_____

_____

_____

What are some key takeaways from your reading this week?

_____

_____

_____

_____

_____

_____

_____

_____

Record your favorite verses from your reading this week:

....

....

....

....

....

....

....

....

....

Write a prayer inspired by what you read and learned this week:

....

....

....

....

....

....

....

....

....

....

WEEK 32

Date ....

Cite the Scripture you read this week:

....

....

....

....

....

....

....

....

How did your reading this week make you feel?

....

....

....

....

....

....

....

....

What lessons did you learn, and how can you apply them to
your life?

_____

_____

_____

_____

_____

_____

_____

What are some key takeaways from your reading this week?

_____

_____

_____

_____

_____

_____

_____

_____

Record your favorite verses from your reading this week:

_____

_____

_____

_____

_____

_____

_____

Write a prayer inspired by what you read and learned this week:

_____

_____

_____

_____

_____

_____

_____

_____

For Inspiration: **Exodus 16:21**

WEEK 33

Date ....

Cite the Scripture you read this week:

....

....

....

....

....

....

....

....

How did your reading this week make you feel?

....

....

....

....

....

....

....

....

....

....

What lessons did you learn, and how can you apply them to your life?

....

....

....

....

....

....

....

What are some key takeaways from your reading this week?

....

....

....

....

....

....

....

....

Record your favorite verses from your reading this week:

....

....

....

....

....

....

....

....

Write a prayer inspired by what you read and learned this week:

....

....

....

....

....

....

....

....

....

WEEK 34

Date ....

Cite the Scripture you read this week:

....

....

....

....

....

....

....

How did your reading this week make you feel?

....

....

....

....

....

....

....

What lessons did you learn, and how can you apply them to
your life?

_____

_____

_____

_____

_____

_____

_____

What are some key takeaways from your reading this week?

_____

_____

_____

_____

_____

_____

_____

_____

Record your favorite verses from your reading this week:

....

....

....

....

....

....

....

....

Write a prayer inspired by what you read and learned this week:

....

....

....

....

....

....

....

....

....

WEEK 35

Date ....

Cite the Scripture you read this week:

....

....

....

....

....

....

....

....

How did your reading this week make you feel?

....

....

....

....

....

....

....

....

....

What lessons did you learn, and how can you apply them to your life?

....

....

....

....

....

....

....

What are some key takeaways from your reading this week?

....

....

....

....

....

....

....

....

Record your favorite verses from your reading this week:

....

....

....

....

....

....

....

....

Write a prayer inspired by what you read and learned this week:

....

....

....

....

....

....

....

....

....

....

WEEK 36

Date ....

Cite the Scripture you read this week:

....

....

....

....

....

....

....

How did your reading this week make you feel?

....

....

....

....

....

....

....

What lessons did you learn, and how can you apply them to your life?

....

....

....

....

....

....

....

What are some key takeaways from your reading this week?

....

....

....

....

....

....

....

....

Record your favorite verses from your reading this week:

....

....

....

....

....

....

....

....

Write a prayer inspired by what you read and learned this week:

....

....

....

....

....

....

....

....

WEEK 37

Date ....

Cite the Scripture you read this week:

_____

_____

_____

_____

_____

_____

_____

_____

How did your reading this week make you feel?

_____

_____

_____

_____

_____

_____

_____

_____

_____

What lessons did you learn, and how can you apply them to your life?

....

....

....

....

....

....

....

....

What are some key takeaways from your reading this week?

....

....

....

....

....

....

....

....

Record your favorite verses from your reading this week:

_____

_____

_____

_____

_____

_____

_____

_____

Write a prayer inspired by what you read and learned this week:

_____

_____

_____

_____

_____

_____

_____

_____

_____

_____

WEEK 38

Date ....

Cite the Scripture you read this week:

_____

_____

_____

_____

_____

_____

_____

How did your reading this week make you feel?

_____

_____

_____

_____

_____

_____

_____

_____

What lessons did you learn, and how can you apply them to
your life?

....

....

....

....

....

....

....

What are some key takeaways from your reading this week?

....

....

....

....

....

....

....

....

Record your favorite verses from your reading this week:

....

....

....

....

....

....

....

....

Write a prayer inspired by what you read and learned this week:

....

....

....

....

....

....

....

....

....

WEEK 39

Date ....

Cite the Scripture you read this week:

....

....

....

....

....

....

....

....

How did your reading this week make you feel?

....

....

....

....

....

....

....

....

....

What lessons did you learn, and how can you apply them to your life?

_____

_____

_____

_____

_____

_____

_____

What are some key takeaways from your reading this week?

_____

_____

_____

_____

_____

_____

_____

_____

Record your favorite verses from your reading this week:

_____

_____

_____

_____

_____

_____

_____

_____

Write a prayer inspired by what you read and learned this week:

_____

_____

_____

_____

_____

_____

_____

_____

_____

For Inspiration: 1 Kings 18:21

WEEK 40

Date ....

Cite the Scripture you read this week:

....

....

....

....

....

....

....

....

How did your reading this week make you feel?

....

....

....

....

....

....

....

....

....

What lessons did you learn, and how can you apply them to your life?

....

....

....

....

....

....

....

What are some key takeaways from your reading this week?

....

....

....

....

....

....

....

....

Record your favorite verses from your reading this week:

....

....

....

....

....

....

....

Write a prayer inspired by what you read and learned this week:

....

....

....

....

....

....

....

....

For Inspiration: **Esther 4:14**

WEEK 41

Date ....

Cite the Scripture you read this week:

....

....

....

....

....

....

....

....

How did your reading this week make you feel?

....

....

....

....

....

....

....

....

....

What lessons did you learn, and how can you apply them to your life?

....

....

....

....

....

....

....

What are some key takeaways from your reading this week?

....

....

....

....

....

....

....

....

Record your favorite verses from your reading this week:

....

....

....

....

....

....

....

....

Write a prayer inspired by what you read and learned this week:

....

....

....

....

....

....

....

....

....

WEEK 42

Date

Cite the Scripture you read this week:

How did your reading this week make you feel?

What lessons did you learn, and how can you apply them to your life?

....

....

....

....

....

....

....

What are some key takeaways from your reading this week?

....

....

....

....

....

....

....

Record your favorite verses from your reading this week:

....

....

....

....

....

....

....

Write a prayer inspired by what you read and learned this week:

....

....

....

....

....

....

....

....

WEEK 43

Date ....

Cite the Scripture you read this week:

....

....

....

....

....

....

....

....

How did your reading this week make you feel?

....

....

....

....

....

....

....

....

....

What lessons did you learn, and how can you apply them to your life?

....

....

....

....

....

....

....

What are some key takeaways from your reading this week?

....

....

....

....

....

....

....

....

Record your favorite verses from your reading this week:

....

....

....

....

....

....

....

Write a prayer inspired by what you read and learned this week:

....

....

....

....

....

....

....

....

....

For Inspiration: Proverbs 31:20

WEEK 44

Date ....

Cite the Scripture you read this week:

....

....

....

....

....

....

....

....

How did your reading this week make you feel?

....

....

....

....

....

....

....

....

What lessons did you learn, and how can you apply them to your life?

....
....
....
....
....
....
....

What are some key takeaways from your reading this week?

....
....
....
....
....
....
....
....

Record your favorite verses from your reading this week:

....

....

....

....

....

....

....

....

Write a prayer inspired by what you read and learned this week:

....

....

....

....

....

....

....

....

WEEK 45

Date ....

Cite the Scripture you read this week:

....
....
....
....
....
....
....

How did your reading this week make you feel?

....
....
....
....
....
....
....
....

What lessons did you learn, and how can you apply them to
your life?

....

....

....

....

....

....

....

What are some key takeaways from your reading this week?

....

....

....

....

....

....

....

....

Record your favorite verses from your reading this week:

....

....

....

....

....

....

....

....

Write a prayer inspired by what you read and learned this week:

....

....

....

....

....

....

....

....

....

WEEK 46

Date ....

Cite the Scripture you read this week:

....

....

....

....

....

....

....

How did your reading this week make you feel?

....

....

....

....

....

....

....

....

....

What lessons did you learn, and how can you apply them to your life?

....

....

....

....

....

....

....

What are some key takeaways from your reading this week?

....

....

....

....

....

....

....

Record your favorite verses from your reading this week:

....

....

....

....

....

....

....

....

Write a prayer inspired by what you read and learned this week:

....

....

....

....

....

....

....

....

WEEK 47

Date ....

Cite the Scripture you read this week:

....

....

....

....

....

....

....

....

How did your reading this week make you feel?

....

....

....

....

....

....

....

....

....

What lessons did you learn, and how can you apply them to your life?

....

....

....

....

....

....

....

What are some key takeaways from your reading this week?

....

....

....

....

....

....

....

....

Record your favorite verses from your reading this week:

....

....

....

....

....

....

....

....

Write a prayer inspired by what you read and learned this week:

....

....

....

....

....

....

....

....

For Inspiration: 1 Corinthians 11:1

WEEK 48

Date ....

Cite the Scripture you read this week:

....

....

....

....

....

....

....

How did your reading this week make you feel?

....

....

....

....

....

....

....

....

What lessons did you learn, and how can you apply them to your life?

_____
_____
_____
_____
_____
_____
_____

What are some key takeaways from your reading this week?

_____
_____
_____
_____
_____
_____
_____
_____

Record your favorite verses from your reading this week:

_____

_____

_____

_____

_____

_____

_____

_____

Write a prayer inspired by what you read and learned this week:

_____

_____

_____

_____

_____

_____

_____

_____

_____

WEEK 49

Date ....

Cite the Scripture you read this week:

....
....
....
....
....
....
....

How did your reading this week make you feel?

....
....
....
....
....
....
....
....

What lessons did you learn, and how can you apply them to your life?

....

....

....

....

....

....

....

What are some key takeaways from your reading this week?

....

....

....

....

....

....

....

....

Record your favorite verses from your reading this week:

....

....

....

....

....

....

....

....

Write a prayer inspired by what you read and learned this week:

....

....

....

....

....

....

....

....

....

WEEK 50

Date ....

Cite the Scripture you read this week:

....

....

....

....

....

....

....

How did your reading this week make you feel?

....

....

....

....

....

....

....

What lessons did you learn, and how can you apply them to your life?

....
....
....
....
....
....
....
....

What are some key takeaways from your reading this week?

....
....
....
....
....
....
....
....

Record your favorite verses from your reading this week:

....

....

....

....

....

....

....

Write a prayer inspired by what you read and learned this week:

....

....

....

....

....

....

....

....

WEEK 51

Date ....

Cite the Scripture you read this week:

....

....

....

....

....

....

....

....

How did your reading this week make you feel?

....

....

....

....

....

....

....

....

....

....

What lessons did you learn, and how can you apply them to your life?

What are some key takeaways from your reading this week?

Record your favorite verses from your reading this week:

....

....

....

....

....

....

....

....

Write a prayer inspired by what you read and learned this week:

....

....

....

....

....

....

....

....

....

WEEK 52

Date ....

Cite the Scripture you read this week:

....
....
....
....
....
....
....

How did your reading this week make you feel?

....
....
....
....
....
....
....
....

What lessons did you learn, and how can you apply them to your life?

....

....

....

....

....

....

....

What are some key takeaways from your reading this week?

....

....

....

....

....

....

....

Record your favorite verses from your reading this week:

Write a prayer inspired by what you read and learned this week:

ACKNOWLEDGMENTS

I want to thank my amazing parents for always supporting me, from the time I was a little girl until now. You have been constant examples of using your gifts to edify the Body of Christ.

To my husband, Dr. Brent, for pushing me to stretch beyond my comfort zone and encouraging me when I wanted to quit.

To my children, Laija and Bryant, for allowing me to show you that you can truly do all things through Christ who gives you strength. Also, for giving me the time I needed to produce such an important book.

ABOUT THE AUTHOR

LaJena James is a speaker, author, and coach for Christian women and girls. She is a native of Louisiana and the CEO of Patty's Pearls School of Etiquette, which teaches young women life and social skills, character education, and all things etiquette.

LaJena has served in education for more than fifteen years. It was in this profession that she found her passion for helping others overcome daily challenges by providing practical tools that help them better manage their days, build healthy relationships with others, and handle conflict.

She also enjoys teaching Christian women how to define their identity in Christ and activate their purpose through her Designed for More coaching program.

She is the author of *Lamp and Light: Navigating Christian Topics through the Word of God*. Learn more at LaJenaJames.com.